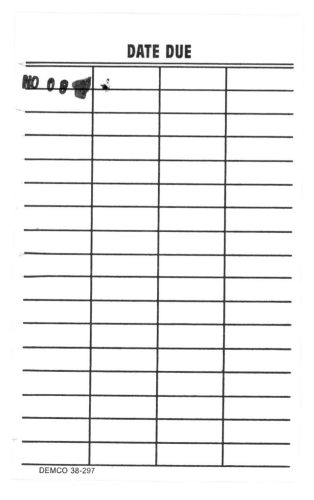

DATE DUE

NO 0 8			

DEMCO 38-297

America's Founding Fathers

GOUVERNEUR MORRIS

Creating a Nation

Samuel Willard Crompton

Enslow Publishers, Inc.

40 Industrial Road   PO Box 38
Box 398   Aldershot
Berkeley Heights, NJ 07922   Hants GU12 6BP
USA   UK

http://www.enslow.com

Library of Congress Cataloging-in-Publication Data

Crompton, Samuel Willard.
    Gouverneur Morris: Creating a Nation/Samuel Willard Crompton.
       p. cm.—(America's founding fathers)
    Summary: Describes the life of Gouverneur Morris, who edited the
final version of the United States Constitution, served as minister to
France, and was instrumental in the establishment of our national
coinage system and in the planning of the Erie Canal.
    Includes bibliographical references and index.
    ISBN 0-7660-2213-7
    1. Morris, Gouverneur, 1752-1816—Juvenile literature.
2. Statesmen—United States—Biography—Juvenile literature.
3. Legislators—New York (State)—Biography—Juvenile literature.
4. United States—History—Revolution, 1775–1783—Biography—
Juvenile literature. 5. New York (State)—History—Revolution,
1775–1783—Biography—Juvenile literature. 6. United States—Politics
and government—1775-1783—Juvenile literature. 7. United States—
Politics and government—1783-1789—Juvenile literature. [1. Morris,
Gouverneur, 1752-1816. 2. Statesmen. 3. Legislators. 4. New York
(State)—History—Revolution, 1775-1783. 5. United States—Politics and
government—1775-1783. 6. United States—Politics and government—
1783-1789.] I. Title. II. Series.
E302.6.M7C76 2004
973.4'092—dc21

                                          2003002402

Printed in the United States of America

10 9 8 7 6 5 4 3 2 1

To Our Readers: We have done our best to make sure all Internet Addresses in
this book were active and appropriate when we went to press. However, the author
and the publisher have no control over and assume no liability for the material
available on those Internet sites or on other Web sites they may link to. Any com-
ments or suggestions can be sent by e-mail to comments@enslow.com or to the
address on the back cover.

Illustration Credits: *American Historical Illustrations and Emblems*,
Published by Dover Publications, Inc., in 1988, pp. 23, 90; Clipart.com,
pp. 4–5, 7, 11, 15, 21, 70, 86, 87, 88, 95, 98, 103; *Dictionary of American
Portraits*, Published by Dover Publications, Inc., in 1967, pp. 10
(left/right), 29, 48, 64, 80, 82 (right), 91, 100 (right); Enslow
Publishers, Inc., pp. 13, 28 (map), 49, 102; June Ponte, p. 1; Library of
Congress, pp. 8, 20, 30, 34, 44, 47, 67, 93, 100 (left), 110, 112–113;
National Archives, pp. 2–3, 19, 22, 26, 28 (background), 31, 32, 39, 42,
54, 71, 81, 82 (left); Courtesy of the Pennsylvania Academy of the Fine
Arts, Philadelphia. Bequest of Richard Ashhurst, p. 50.

Cover Illustration: Corel Corporation (background); June Ponte
(portrait).

Contents

The year 1777 was sometimes called the Year of the Hangman. It proved to be an important year in the struggle for American independence.

Year of the Hangman

SOME PEOPLE LIVING in 1777 called this period the Year of the Three Sevens. Others called it the Year of the Hangman, because each of the three sevens resembled a gallows—a structure from which people are hanged. Whatever it was named, 1777 was a critical time in America.

During the previous year on July 4, 1776, the American colonies had declared their independence from Great Britain and its king. Delegates from the colonies had come together during the Second Continental Congress to adopt the Declaration of Independence. This document blamed British oppression for the colonial desire to be free from British rule. For years, England had unfairly taxed and passed laws against the best interest of the colonies.

After Americans issued the Declaration of Independence, the American Revolution accelerated. Americans were forced to win their freedom from England through many bloody battles and strategic military moves. In 1777, the American cause seemed in great doubt. British troops had defeated the American forces repeatedly and patriotic spirits were tested. Would 1777 be the year that the patriots ended up at the gallows?

Fort Ticonderoga

In 1777, England had devised a plan for three of its forces to meet at Albany, New York. By occupying the Hudson River and its valley, the British troops would split the rebellious colonies in half. The four New England colonies—New Hampshire, Massachusetts, Rhode Island, and Connecticut—would be split off from the other nine.

On July 4, 1777, British general John Burgoyne placed a cannon on top of Mount Defiance, overlooking Fort Ticonderoga located at a narrow spot on Lake Champlain. Fort Ticonderoga was one of the strongest American defenses. It was seen as vital to the safety of New York. Burgoyne's clever move foiled the American position. American general Arthur

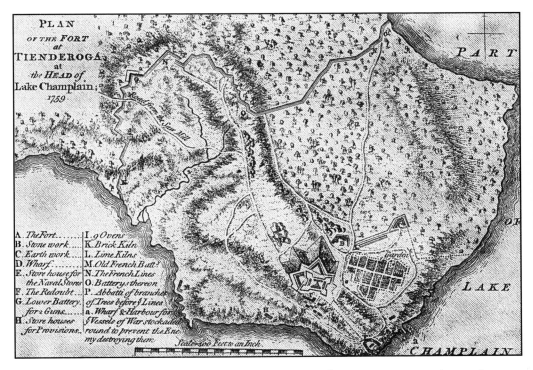

During the American Revolution, Fort Ticonderoga was strategic to the protection of New York from British invasion. This sketch shows an early plan for Fort Ticonderoga.

St. Clair was forced to evacuate his men on July 5. Burgoyne believed his strategy had weakened American resistance. When the news of Ticonderoga's fall arrived in London, King George III exclaimed, "I have beaten them! I have beaten all the Americans!"[1]

Assessing the Situation

On July 10, 1777, just five days after Ticonderoga's fall, Gouverneur Morris traveled north to investigate the American situation.[2] Morris was a member of the Provincial Congress of New York—an assembly organized by the patriots to help govern New York during its transition from colony to independence. Morris arrived at Albany on July 14 accompanied by Abraham Yates, another member of the Provincial Congress. He quickly moved on to Fort Edward, where the Hudson River turns to the west, two days later. There, he met with General St. Clair and General Philip Schuyler, who had overall command of the American defenses in this area.

Gouverneur Morris was a member of the New York Provincial Congress in the summer of 1777.

Morris predicted danger for the Americans if British forces advanced from Fort Ticonderoga to Albany. He knew that the patriots at Fort Edward must hold the British back. His keen eye had taken in the situation. The Hudson River valley, which was the British objective, was open, rolling farmland. If the British reached the valley, they would easily spread through it and conquer much of the New York colony. But if the British could be held north of Albany, the forest country there might prevent them from reaching their goal. Morris already saw what must be done to prevent another American loss. He advised General Schuyler and the Council of Safety of New York, "I will venture to say that if we . . . leave nothing but a wilderness to the enemy, their progress must be impeded by obstacles, which it is not in human nature to surmount."[3]

Stop the British!

A few days later, large groups of Americans went north from Fort Edward. They concentrated their energy on the twenty-mile section between Wood Creek and the bend in the Hudson River. The Americans cut down trees to block passage through the forest. They also destroyed bridges, generally making the wilderness road even worse than it had been before. Would Morris's idea be enough to stop the British advance?

Twenty miles north of Fort Edward, British general Burgoyne was slow in taking action against the Americans making a mess of the forest pathways. While the Americans were creating obstacles to stop the British advance, Burgoyne could have sent his fast-moving infantry soldiers forward. They could have picked their way through the woods and reached Fort Edward in a matter of days. But Burgoyne wanted to travel in style.

A man of London society, Burgoyne wanted to bring his baggage wagons with him. To accommodate these wagons, he had his men rebuild all the bridges and pull trees from his path. Burgoyne took twenty days to cover the twenty miles! By the time he reached Fort Edward, the American forces south of that point had grown stronger. The forest obstacles, in addition to

Generals Arthur St. Clair (left) and Philip Schuyler (right) commanded American defenses near the Hudson River valley during the American Revolution.

In 1777, obstacles constructed by American colonists prevented British troops from advancing to the Hudson River valley.

Burgoyne's vanity, had prevented a British advance to the Hudson River valley.

Gouverneur Morris was, like Burgoyne, a man born to wealth and privilege. But Morris, unlike Burgoyne, knew the American landscape. Morris's idea had used that landscape to gain twenty days for the American forces to build up. These twenty days proved invaluable. Burgoyne would not reach Albany, and 1777 would not be the Year of the Hangman for the patriot cause in America.

Young Aristocrat

GOUVERNEUR WAS BORN on January 31, 1752, on the family estate called Morrisania. It was located in what is now the southern part of the Bronx, New York. Morrisania was an estate of about nineteen hundred acres. Few of the founding fathers grew up with as much privilege and comfort as the young Gouverneur Morris.

Gouverneur's father was Lewis Morris, Jr., and his mother was Sarah Gouverneur. Both families had been in the New York colony for several generations. Gouverneur was Sarah's third child. He had two older sisters, and later he had two younger ones. He also had three half-brothers

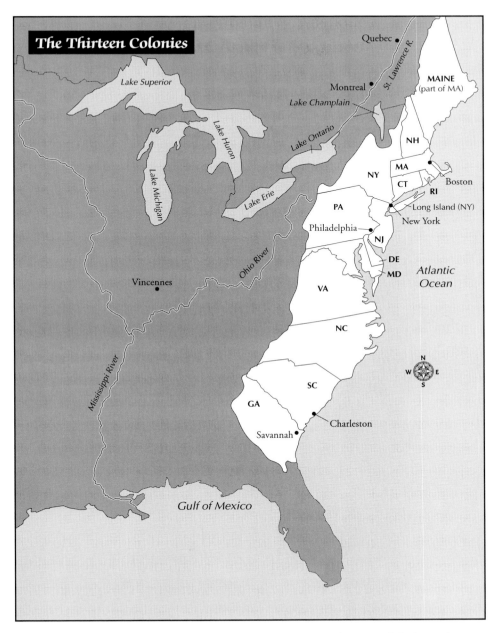

The Thirteen Colonies

Lake Superior

Lake Huron

Lake Michigan

Lake Erie

Lake Ontario

Lake Champlain

St. Lawrence R.

Quebec

Montreal

MAINE
(part of MA)

NH

NY

MA

CT

Boston

RI

Long Island (NY)

New York

PA

Philadelphia

NJ

DE

MD

Atlantic
Ocean

Ohio River

Vincennes

VA

NC

Mississippi River

SC

GA

Charleston

Savannah

Gulf of Mexico

N
W E
S

This map depicts the thirteen original colonies and some of their major cities. Gouverneur Morris was born in the colony of New York.

and a half-sister, all of whom had been born during his father's first marriage to Tryntje Staats. His half-brothers—Richard, Lewis III, and Staats Long Morris—were intended to inherit the family estate.

The Morris family was one of the wealthiest and most distinguished in all of New York. Gouverneur's grandfather, Lewis Morris, Sr., had received manorial rights to Morrisania in 1697.[1] This meant that he could hold his own court, try his subjects, and establish all the rules to be followed at the manor. These rights passed to Lewis Morris, Jr., and then to Staats Long Morris over the course of time.

The Morris family held slaves. Gouverneur's great-grandfather, Richard Morris, had emigrated from Barbados around 1671. Richard Morris had brought Africans with him as slaves. By 1740, Lewis Morris, Sr., was probably the largest slave owner in the entire New York colony.[2] Gouverneur grew up in the presence of slaves, but he learned to detest the institution of slavery.

Gouverneur's tutors recognized that he was very bright. They often commented, however, that he did not spend as much time studying as they would have wished. Gouverneur was a playful child—very happy outdoors and known for his pranks.

Slavery in the Thirteen Colonies

African-American slaves lived in all thirteen American colonies. The African Americans in the northern colonies were often called "servants," but their true status was that of slaves. The middle colonies, including New York, had a slave population, but the institution of slavery did not thrive there as it did in the South. In the southern colonies, tobacco and cotton—crops that required many fieldworkers—were important parts of the economy. African-American slaves became a source of labor for Southern plantations.

Slave labor was used for cotton production in southern colonies.

Young Gouverneur was at a private school in New Rochelle, New York, when his father died in 1762. Lewis Morris, Jr., left a curious will. He asked that no newspaper or magazine print any news of his death. The bulk of his estate went to his sons Richard, Lewis III, and Staats Long Morris. Sarah Gouverneur was to have possession of Morrisania as long as she lived. Gouverneur was to receive two thousand British pounds. This was no small amount, but limited considering what went to his older brothers. When it came to the matter of Gouverneur's education, Lewis Morris, Jr., was quite explicit. He wanted Gouverneur to receive an excellent education. The will directed that the estate should pay for any schooling, as long as Yale was excluded from consideration. Lewis Morris, Jr., made it quite plain that he detested Yale. In the fall of 1764, Gouverneur entered King's College (now Columbia University) in New York City.[3]

Higher Education

Gouverneur was one of eight class members who entered King's College that autumn. His fellow classmates were from the same social class: New York's richest.

Though he was expected to graduate in the spring of 1767, Gouverneur's graduation was postponed for a full year because of an accident. While on a ladder, scalding water had been poured onto his left arm. The arm was burned so severely that doctors feared gangrene—the death of body tissues caused by a loss of blood to areas of the body—but the arm was saved. Gouverneur had to return to Morrisania for a number of months to recover. By the time he returned, it was clear that he would have to spend an extra year at King's College.

The extra academic year was no hardship for Gouverneur, who delighted in learning. He was an excellent student who absorbed material very quickly. He earned his best marks in Latin and French.

When graduation arrived in the spring of 1768, sixteen-year-old Gouverneur was selected to deliver the graduation speech. A small crowd gathered at St. Paul's Chapel in New York City on May 17, 1768. Seven students took their degrees that day. Morris's speech, entitled "Wit and Beauty," helped spread his reputation as a powerful orator, or public speaker.

The Law

After graduation, Morris studied law in New York City under the direction of Judge William Smith, who was regarded as one of the top men in the legal profession. Smith had also written a history of New York.

In 1771, nineteen-year-old Morris was admitted to the bar in New York. This meant that he could now practice law. Morris put in long hours at the office, but also spent many hours socializing at parties. One of his closest friends was fellow lawyer John Jay.

Like Morris, Jay had been tutored in New Rochelle. The two young men made an interesting pair. Morris was the more outgoing of the

Catherine Livingston

During the time that Morris studied law with Judge William Smith, he also experienced the first love of his life. Catherine Livingston, better known as Kitty, was from one of the oldest and most esteemed families of New York. Morris pledged his love to Kitty numerous times in letters, and appealed for some sign of her favor, which she declined to give. It was the first of many romances in Morris's life.[4]

pair. Jay was more reserved, but his wicked sense of humor amused Morris.

London

Like many young men, Morris thought about going to England to refine his manners and learn from the great city of London. He wrote to Judge Smith about what he hoped to gain from traveling across the ocean:

> I hope to form some acquaintances, that may hereafter be of service to me, to model myself after some persons, who cut a figure in the profession of the law, to form my manners and address by the example of the truly polite, to rub off . . . a few of those many barbarisms, which characterize a provincial education.[5]

Smith wrote back three days later. He pointed out that Morris was doing well in New York. He reminded Morris that one of his uncles, Robert

Hunter Morris, had lost almost his entire fortune by spending too much time going back and forth between London and America. The older man's advice was taken. Morris did not venture across the Atlantic to London.

A War Brewing

When the French and Indian War ended in 1763, Great Britain had a huge war debt. The victory against French and American Indian enemies had been costly. King George III looked to the American colonies to help increase England's income. The British Parliament passed numerous laws that helped England's economy, while hurting that of the colonies. First, England passed the Sugar Act of 1764, which placed a tax on molasses and damaged colonial trade.

More offensive to colonists was the Stamp Act of 1765. This act made it necessary to buy a British stamp for every piece of printed paper used. These stamps proved that the tax had been paid, and were needed on all documents. The Townshend Acts of 1767 placed duties on lead, paper, paint, glass, and tea.

John Jay was one of Gouverneur Morris's closest friends.

The colonies and Great Britain were divided over a question of power. The British government believed that it could tax the Americans at will, while American colonists believed that they could only be taxed with their consent, in the form of representatives in Parliament. Because they did not have representatives, colonists believed laws passed against them by Parliament were unjustified.

The colonists were growing weary of British rule. They felt that they were being exploited by the mother country and deserved the same rights as people living in England. By the 1770s, tensions between Great Britain and the colonies had come to a head. On March 5, 1770, seven British soldiers fired into a crowd of people in Boston, Massachusetts. Five colonists died. This incident, which became known as the Boston Massacre, was a small glimpse of the violence to come.

Under the Stamp Act of 1765, colonists needed to purchase a British stamp for every piece of printed paper used.

On December 16, 1773, about two hundred colonists dressed as American Indians boarded British ships in the Boston Harbor. These men threw all the tea into the

During the Boston Massacre, British soldiers fired into a crowd of American colonists. This event added to the anti-British sentiment sweeping through the American colonies.

water. The Boston Tea Party, as it was later called, demonstrated the rebellious feelings toward England spreading throughout the colonies. After the Boston Tea Party, King George decided to teach the colonists a lesson. Parliament passed the Coercive Acts, which closed the port of Boston and forbade the people of Massachusetts to hold town meetings. Trade within the city suffered. When

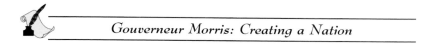

In 1773, American colonists boarded British ships in Boston Harbor and threw tea into the water. This incident became known as the Boston Tea Party.

the news of these repressive measures reached America, the colonists called them the "Intolerable Acts."

Boston was the city most affected by the Coercive Acts, but people from other colonies were also concerned. Merchants and farmers from as far as Virginia sent food and clothing to help the people of Boston. There were also many political meetings in other cities, one of which Gouverneur Morris attended. Up to this point in his life, Morris had shown little interest in politics. But by 1774,

Morris saw that a violent break from England could become a reality.

Fraunces Tavern

In 1774, Gouverneur Morris went to a meeting that was held to address the colonists' discontent toward England. The meeting took place at the Fraunces Tavern in Manhattan, the southern part of New York City.

The Fraunces Tavern had been owned by Samuel Fraunces since 1762. In the eighteenth century, taverns were gathering places, where

Fraunces Tavern in New York was the setting for many political debates prior to and during the American Revolution.

community members met to discuss business, local news, or politics. By the 1770s, the Fraunces Tavern was the scene of many meetings to discuss the growing unrest in the colonies.

The meeting that Morris attended there on May 19, 1774, was one such gathering. Many at the meeting supported the idea of independence from Great Britain. Morris was not confident that revolution was the best choice. In a letter written the next day to John Penn of Philadelphia, Morris declared:

> I see, and I see it with fear and trembling, that if the disputes with Britain continue, we shall be under the worst of all possible dominions. We shall be under the domination of a riotous mob.[6]

Morris feared that the colonists might not be able to govern themselves. No answer from John Penn is recorded.

Morris was an aristocrat, or a member of the upper class. He was in favor of law and order under a noble government. But what was he to do if most of his fellow New Yorkers decided they were under the rule of unfair government? At this point, Morris was not in favor of revolution against England. But by the spring of 1775, Morris's life would take a different course. Morris would become a patriot.

New York Patriot

IN SEPTEMBER 1774, a convention of delegates from the American colonies met in Philadelphia. This convention was called the First Continental Congress. The delegates wanted to limit England's control over the colonies and petition the king for fair treatment—not independence. The convention agreed to meet again in May 1775 if Britain did not change its policies.

The Battle of Lexington and Concord

In early 1775, Parliament made it legal for British troops in Boston to shoot or arrest rebels in an effort to stop colonial uprisings. Patriots learned about these orders and fled Boston.

On the night of April 18, 1775, British soldiers began marching toward Concord, Massachusetts, to capture arms and gunpowder stored there by patriots. The British troops reached the town of Lexington, on the way to Concord, on April 19. American militiamen were waiting for them. Shots were fired and several colonists were

The Battle of Lexington was the first exchange of shots between American colonists and British soldiers during the American Revolution.

killed. The British continued on to Concord, where more than three hundred American militiamen were waiting. The British then turned back toward Boston. Along the way, patriots fired at them from behind trees and fences.

News of the Battles of Lexington and Concord arrived in New York City on Sunday, April 23. Many New Yorkers saw the post rider who galloped down Broadway, crying out that the American Revolution had begun.[1]

Morris now decided to side with the patriot cause. Biographer Max M. Mintz commented that Morris "was young, and the Revolution was in one sense a young man's movement."[2] Whatever his motivation was at the time, he never looked back once he joined the patriot cause. However, there would always be some skeptics, who claimed that Morris was a closet Loyalist. His mother, one sister, two brothers-in-law, and one half-brother were Loyalists.[3]

Life in New York was not like it was in Boston. There had always been a substantial number of merchants and officeholders there, who were loyal to Great Britain. Also, New York had never been closed off from overseas trade, like Boston had. As a result, the revolutionary movement gained ground in New York slowly— at least at first.

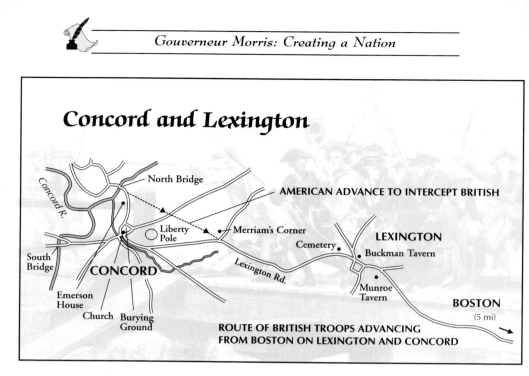

Concord and Lexington

North Bridge

Concord R.

AMERICAN ADVANCE TO INTERCEPT BRITISH

Liberty Pole

Merriam's Corner

Cemetery

LEXINGTON

Buckman Tavern

South Bridge

CONCORD

Lexington Rd.

Emerson House

Munroe Tavern

BOSTON
(5 mi)

Church   Burying Ground

ROUTE OF BRITISH TROOPS ADVANCING FROM BOSTON ON LEXINGTON AND CONCORD

In 1775, the important Battles of Lexington and Concord, in Massachusetts, began the American Revolution.

Provincial Congress of New York

On May 22, 1775, Gouverneur Morris was elected as a delegate to New York's Provincial Congress.[4] John Jay and Richard Montgomery were among his fellow legislators, or lawmakers. These men would have the authority to shape New York's course during the American Revolution and its laws for some time to come.

Just one month into its existence, the Provincial Congress faced a dilemma. On June 25, 1775, George Washington, who had been chosen as the new commander in chief of the

Continental Army, was due to visit New York on his way to Boston. Coincidentally, the British royal governor, William Tryon, was expected to visit on the same day.

New York was not as far along as Boston was in its revolutionary feelings. The New York legislators decided to appease the leader of the Continental Army and the British royal governor at the same time. One committee of the Provincial Congress would meet with Washington and give him a tour of New York. A second committee would do the same for Tryon.[5]

Gouverneur Morris was a member of the committee that greeted Washington. It was the first meeting between these two men, who

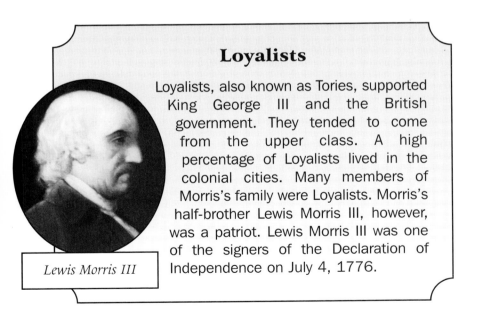

Loyalists

Loyalists, also known as Tories, supported King George III and the British government. They tended to come from the upper class. A high percentage of Loyalists lived in the colonial cities. Many members of Morris's family were Loyalists. Morris's half-brother Lewis Morris III, however, was a patriot. Lewis Morris III was one of the signers of the Declaration of Independence on July 4, 1776.

Lewis Morris III

would continue their relationship for the next twenty-four years.

The "Fourteenth Colony"

In July 1775, Gouverneur Morris was one of the legislators in the Provincial Congress of New York who considered an American invasion of Canada. Canada was governed by Great Britain. Revolutionary Americans had sent letters and pamphlets to Canada urging the Canadians to join in the patriot cause. Many Americans believed it would be good to attack and take Canada. Then the British would have fewer bases there from which to attack the American colonies. Also, America would hold another bargaining chip when the time came for peace negotiations.

George Washington met Gouverneur Morris in 1775. This was the beginning of a lifetime friendship.

Richard Montgomery led the American forces north from Albany. Benedict Arnold led American troops from Massachusetts, through Maine, and to Quebec. Montgomery and Arnold joined forces near Quebec. On the night of December 31, 1775, the Americans launched their attack on the city.

This attack failed. Montgomery was killed, and Arnold was wounded in the leg. The American attempt to make Canada the "Fourteenth Colony" was a failure. Canada remained under British control.

At almost the same time as the failure at Quebec, twenty-five-year-old American colonel Henry Knox was dragging cannons from Fort Ticonderoga in upstate New York to the

During the Battle of Quebec, an American attack on Canada from Albany, American military leader Richard Montgomery (center, being held) was fatally wounded.

American encampment around Boston. Using these cannons, General Washington forced the British to evacuate Boston on March 17, 1776.

The British Seize New York City

By the late spring of 1776, it was clear that the British wanted to take New York City. Because of its splendid location and harbor, the city would make a great base for the British forces. Knowing this, General Washington brought most of the Continental Army to New York. The American troops were stationed at points all around the

Signing of the Declaration of Independence

The Declaration of Independence

The Continental Congress approved the Declaration of Independence on July 4, 1776. Written by Thomas Jefferson of Virginia, this document listed the many abuses committed by King George III against the colonies. With the acceptance of the Declaration of Independence, the thirteen colonies now officially became independent states.

city, including Brooklyn and Long Island. But the American cause was about to suffer heavy military losses.

Although General Washington defended it to the best of his ability, the British entered New York City on September 17, 1776. Washington and the remnants of the Continental Army went north. After two embarrassing losses at Fort Washington and Fort Lee, many Americans escaped to New Jersey to regroup. It was a dark time for the American cause.

The British advance had forced the Provincial Congress to leave Manhattan. The Congress was now located at Kingston, on the west side of the Hudson River, about fifty miles north of New York City. There, the delegates discussed the military crisis and the need to create a New York Constitution.

During this critical time, Morris was still a member of the Provincial Congress of New York. Morris did, however, take an unofficial leave of absence. During this critical period for the patriots, Morris spent nearly two months living with relatives in the New Jersey area. Morris was unembarrassed by his conduct. Some of his fellow delegates, though, were both embarrassed and upset by his behavior.[6]

In the fall of 1776, New York City was in the hands of British forces. Here, British ships occupy the harbor and British troops line the shore.

Morris returned to his duties in early winter of 1776–1777. The Provincial Congress of New York came together to write a constitution.

A New York Constitution

In 1776, Gouverneur Morris was a member of the committee appointed to draft a constitution for New York. This was an important first in the American experience. There had been charters and documents before, but the king of England

and Parliament had issued them. Now Morris and a handful of legislators—including John Jay—had the opportunity to write what would become New York State's first constitution.

No state had devised a Constitution to replace the former laws under the British government. Morris and the other committee members intended to write the document, while all sixty-six members of the Provincial Congress gathered to hear the results.

John Jay was selected as the most level-headed man for the purpose of writing the constitution. Jay labored in semiseclusion for some weeks, and then went to Kingston where he presented his writing on March 12, 1777.

Jay was a cautious man. Given the time and opportunity to write what could have been a daring, revolutionary document, Jay instead stayed close to the model provided by the former British government.

Jay's proposed constitution called for a governor, who was to be elected for a term of three years.[7] A legislative branch—composed of an upper house called the Senate and a lower house called the Assembly—was also suggested. The legislative branch would pass laws. The Senate would have twenty-four members, while the Assembly would have seventy members. Senators were to be elected on a rotational basis, with some being voted in or out every four years. The Assemblymen were to be elected every year.[8] Some Americans complained that this constitution echoed the British model too closely.

Jay's plan also called for voting requirements. In order to vote for a member of the Assembly, a voter had to be a male of age. He also had to own property valued at twenty pounds or to pay rent on property that amounted to at least forty shillings per year. In order to vote for Senate members, a voter had to be a male of age, free of debt, and with property valued at least at one hundred pounds. The same requirement applied to voting for the Governor.[9]

Surprisingly, Jay's conservative draft passed with little difficulty. The members of the Provincial Congress debated several items at length. There was general agreement that the governor and two-house legislature, together with the strict voting requirements, were beneficial. Stickier though, for Morris, were two other issues having to do with religion and slavery.

John Jay had inserted a clause that allowed for general religious toleration with an exception concerning Roman Catholics. They were not to be allowed into the state or to become citizens until they swore that the pope had no power in religious matters or to forgive sins that men committed.

Morris and Jay were the best of friends, but Morris disagreed with Jay on this issue. Morris argued for a statute of complete religious toleration, such as the one that the Dutch colony of New Netherland (the former name of New York) had used. Morris and Jay eventually compromised, and the statute did have some limitations for Roman Catholics, but these limitations were less than what had been originally proposed.

In addition to this change, Morris proposed a statute to the constitution that would encourage New York to get rid of slavery at the earliest opportunity. Morris had long been opposed to slavery. This might seem strange coming from a man who had grown up on an estate with fifty slaves, but Morris argued passionately.[10] The vote on this statute failed, however, and New York did not outlaw slavery until 1795.

On April 20, 1777, the members of the Provincial Congress ratified the New York Constitution. It was published in the newspapers on April 22. Morris had helped create the first state constitution in the new nation. It would endure as the law of the land until it was replaced in 1821.

Saratoga

Morris and his colleagues had accomplished a great task. But other challenges loomed on the horizon. Just two months after the Provincial Congress published the new constitution, a British army under General John Burgoyne invaded New York by way of Lake Champlain.

Burgoyne captured Fort Ticonderoga and pressed south toward the Hudson River. Teams of American soldiers cut down trees and destroyed bridges in order to slow the British advance. Their efforts were rewarded in October 1777. Burgoyne and his army were stopped and then trapped by thousands of New York and Vermont militiamen at Saratoga, New York. On October 17, Burgoyne's men—all seven thousand of them—laid down their arms in the first mass British surrender of the war. The American victory at Saratoga ensured that the American Revolution would be a long struggle. It also encouraged European nations to look upon the former American colonies (now the American States) with higher hopes.

Morris was happy to learn of Burgoyne's surrender. Like other Americans, he perceived this as a major turning point in the war. Morris was not on hand to witness the triumph at Saratoga, however. One day before Burgoyne surrendered, Morris helped evacuate the town of Kingston,

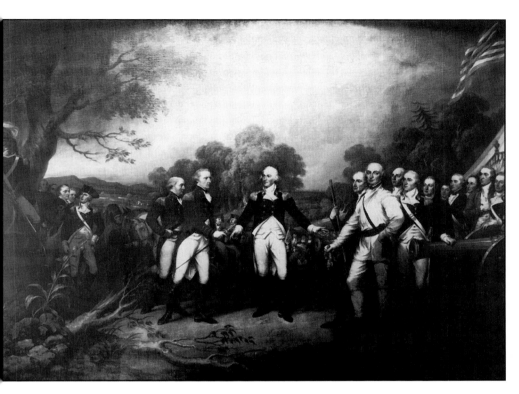

In October 1777, the first mass British surrender during the American Revolution took place when British troops under John Burgoyne laid down their arms in Saratoga, New York.

New York. British general Henry Clinton had sent troops to burn the town.[11]

As the events of the war moved rapidly, Morris's political career advanced, as well. In the fall of 1777, he was elected to serve New York in the Second Continental Congress.[12]

Morris and
Morris

ON JANUARY 20, 1778, Gouverneur Morris arrived at York, Pennsylvania and took his place as a member of the Second Continental Congress. The Continental Congress had moved from Philadelphia to York three months earlier, just before the British captured Philadelphia.

Morris arrived at a time of crisis for the American cause. Although General Burgoyne had surrendered to the Americans in October 1777, General William Howe had taken Philadelphia. General Washington's army was in distress. On the very day he arrived, Morris was named as a member of a committee to consult with Washington over the state of the Continental Army.[1]

Around this time, Morris was introduced to the Marquis de Lafayette, a twenty-year-old French nobleman who had crossed the Atlantic Ocean to assist with the American cause of independence.[2]

Valley Forge

Shortly after arriving to serve the Second Continental Congress, Morris went to Valley Forge, Pennsylvania, where American troops were stationed in shabby winter quarters. For many of the soldiers, there was a lack of warm clothing and shoes. The men also struggled to survive despite a food shortage. More supplies were necessary if Washington's men were going to endure the bitter winter. Many soldiers were dying from malnutrition, exposure to the cold, and such diseases as smallpox and typhoid fever. Morris was to meet with General Washington to discuss the situation.

Morris had spent time with Washington once before, when the general had passed through New York City in 1775. The two men now renewed their acquaintance, and soon had the makings of a genuine friendship. Both men were sincere, devoted patriots from the upper class. There the comparison ended. Washington was

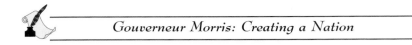

George Washington and a committee of Congress, including Gouverneur Morris, met at Valley Forge to discuss the state of the Continental Army.

serious, while Morris was cheerful. Just the same, the two men got along quite well.

Upon returning from Valley Forge, Morris became a spokesperson for the Continental Army. He convinced the Second Continental Congress to purchase more supplies for American soldiers. These supplies helped the American army make it through the terrible winter at Valley Forge.

Combined with the new training given by Prussian soldier Baron Friedrich Wilhelm Ludolf Gerhard Augustin von Steuben, the American soldiers were in better shape in the spring of 1778 than they had been in the past. Then, on May 2, came the welcome news that France had allied with the Americans against Great Britain. The American victory at Saratoga had persuaded the court of King Louis XVI to take the plunge and enter the war.

Around this time, British peace commissioners arrived to negotiate with the Americans. Concerned over the prospect of fighting a two-front war (one with France and one with the United States), the British wanted to come to a cease-fire with their former colonists. Morris attacked any such notion and persuaded Americans to continue to fight.[3] Victory was now quite possible. The Americans had to stand firm.

Setback

For the next year, Morris was occupied with financial matters. Few members of the Continental Congress had as much confidence in their financial skills as Morris did, even though many of them had been in business for a longer period of time. Morris wanted to put the American finances on a sound footing and to do so in a way that would have the American economy resemble

King Louis XVI was convinced to enter the American Revolution after the American victory at Saratoga, New York.

that of England. A strong merchant marine and the encouragement of trade were also priorities for Morris. He soon, however, found himself removed from Congress.

Morris failed to be reelected in 1779. The major complaint against him was that he had been inattentive to New York's concern about the Hampshire Grants. What is known today as the state of Vermont was bitterly contested between New York on one side and New Hampshire on the other. The Hampshire Grants—as the area was called—became a major concern to the voters in New York. They believed Morris had not done enough to ensure that the land became part of New York State. Therefore, he lost the election and was removed from the Continental Congress, though not from Philadelphia.[4] Morris had become attached to Philadelphia and his many friends in the town.

A Strong Spirit

In May 1780, Morris suffered an accident that changed his life. One day when his carriage was brought to his door, Morris climbed onboard with the horses not tethered, or held by a servant. The horses suddenly took off and threw him to the ground. Morris's left leg was caught in one of the carriage wheels. He suffered broken bones. Taken to the local physicians because his own doctor was out of town, Morris learned that he must suffer the loss of his leg to preserve his life. Morris accepted the news. The leg was cut off below the knee, and Morris spent several months recovering.

Morris rebounded from the loss of his leg. He never asked for sympathy and often asked friends not to worry about his condition. When one friend expressed sorrow, Morris replied, "O, Sir, the loss is much less than you imagine; I shall doubtless be a steadier man with one leg than with two."[5]

Eventually, Morris was fitted with a wooden leg, which he had for the rest of his life. Morris continued to dance, sail, and ride horses. The loss of his leg did nothing to hinder the activity of his mind and spirit.[6]

Congress of the Confederation

The Continental Congress first met in September 1774. It continued to meet until 1781, when the approval of the new Articles of Confederation led to the election of a new legislative body called the Congress of the Confederation. This group operated the U.S. government from March 1, 1781, until March 4, 1789, when it was replaced by the Congress established by the U.S. Constitution.

Gouverneur Morris lost his leg during an accident in 1780. He wore a wooden leg for the rest of his life.

National Finances

In July 1781, Morris was asked to become assistant superintendent of finance for the new country. The invitation came from Superintendent of Finance Robert Morris of Philadelphia. Robert Morris was not related to Gouverneur Morris.[7]

Born in England on January 31, 1735, Robert Morris was seventeen years older than

Gouverneur Morris to the very day. Robert Morris had come to the colonies as a young man and had thrived in the merchant trade. The two men got along well. Robert Morris usually began his letters to Morris with "My Dear Gouverneur," which was more casual than Robert Morris's usual manner of address.[8]

Robert Morris was not related to Gouverneur Morris, but the two were friends and colleagues.

Morris and Morris ran the Finance Office of the United States from a rented store at the corners of Market and Fifth streets in Philadelphia. The salaries offered in their finance positions disappointed both men, but they went about their business with passion. The two men worked long hours, but they kept their spirits up partly through poking fun at themselves and each other. Morris once wrote to Robert:

> If you see the Doctor, tell him that Fatiguing from four in the Morning till eight in the Evening & sleeping only from eleven till three agrees with me much better than all the Prescriptions in all the physical Books in all the Languages of the World.[9]

Many challenges faced the pair. At this time, there were about thirteen different currencies for the thirteen separate states. The expression "not worth a Continental" had emerged, meaning that a note of Continental paper money was not worth anything at all. Morris and Morris set their minds to rectify the situation. Robert Morris was occupied with obtaining loans from foreign powers, particularly France. Gouverneur Morris was researching and writing a proposal for a new mint.

Morris's proposal for a new mint was submitted to Congress in January of 1782. The report suggested that the new American currency be based on the Spanish

Continental paper money was not valued highly because each of the separate thirteen states had thirteen different currencies.

The partnership of Gouverneur Morris (left) and Robert Morris (right) helped improve the finances of the young American nation.

silver dollar, with fractions that would include a bill, a penny, and a quarter of a penny. The congressional committee voted to accept the proposal, but Congress stalled for two years. At that time, it accepted a different proposal, authored by Thomas Jefferson. Jefferson's proposal also emphasized the decimal system, as proposed by Morris, but rejected the quarter unit as too small.[10]

Working together, Morris and Morris also founded the first national bank. On January 7, 1782, the Bank of North America opened its doors in Philadelphia. Gouverneur Morris purchased a share for $400. This purchase made him both a creator of and investor in the new financial system.[11]

Our Friend Gouverneur writes you Political Letters but as he tells you nothing of himself it is just that I tell you, how industrious, how useful he is. His talents and abilities you know they are all faithfully and disinterestedly applied to the Service of His Country. I could do nothing without him and our joint labours do but keep the wheels in motions. With sincere attachment I am my Dear Sir Your Friend and humble Servant

(signed) Robt Morris.[12]

One of the finest testimonies to Gouverneur Morris's ability came in a letter from Robert Morris to John Jay, written on January 7, 1784. Morris finished his letter praising Gouverneur Morris's services to the United States.

Morris released a "Report on Public Credit" on July 29, 1782.[13] Like his fellow statesman Alexander Hamilton, Morris believed that the new United States required a financial footing like that of England. Morris proposed that the U.S. Congress take on the entire war debt of the thirteen states. This way, Morris argued, the government would become responsible for the economy and win the confidence of foreign governments and investors. Morris did not convince Congress on this occasion, but his plan was later taken up by Alexander Hamilton. His idea was accepted by Congress in 1790.

Gouverneur Morris left his position as assistant superintendent of finance in 1785. He temporarily retired to private life. Though he did not know it at the time, Morris was fortunate to leave when he did. His great friend Robert Morris would become embroiled in heavy debts and eventually be confined to debtor's prison.

Family Matters

THE AMERICAN REVOLUTION was won with the campaign that ended at Yorktown, Virginia, in October 1781. British general Charles Cornwallis surrendered with seven thousand of his men. It took another two years for the peace treaty between the United States and England to be negotiated and signed. The American struggle for independence had succeeded.

Morris now had time to look into his own personal affairs. He was still young—only thirty-one years old—and he intended to make his fortune in the world.

Morris also had time to consider important family matters. What would become of his relatives who had remained loyal to King George III? Lewis Morris III, Gouverneur Morris's oldest half-brother, had become a patriot. Richard Morris, the second half-brother, had also joined the patriot cause. The youngest half-brother, Staats Long Morris, had joined the British Army long before the beginning of the American

In October 1781, British forces under Charles Cornwallis, surrendered to American forces at Yorktown, Virginia.

Revolution. Although he was on the losing side, Staats Long Morris had nothing to fear because he lived in England. But what would happen to Morris's mother and loyalist sisters who were in the colonies?

During the American Revolution, Morris had not seen his mother. He was reunited with her in June 1783. He was distressed at the sight of his beloved home of Morrisania. In the autumn of 1776, soon after the British conquest of New York City, the family graves at Morrisania had been plundered. Coffins had been broken into and bones had been tossed about. During the war, the British had quartered a number of soldiers there. They had cut down numerous trees to make planks for ships.[1] The Morris family had suffered as a whole. Morris's sister, her husband, and their eight children were about to move to Nova Scotia, a Canadian province that juts out into the Atlantic Ocean from the mainland. They were Loyalists and were unwelcome in the United States.

Soon after the war was over, Morris embarked on a series of ambitious business deals. He bought land in upstate New York. Morris also explored Virginia for business opportunities. In 1786, Morris had the possibility of owning the estate on which he had grown up, Morrisania.

I sit down to let you know, that I am in this world, though in a remote part of it. I have heard of you, but not from you, since I left Morrisania; neither have I had the satisfaction to learn, that, of the many letters I have written, you have ever received one. It would give me infinite pleasure to hear of my friends, yourself in particular, but since it is my lot to know no more than the burthen of general report, I must be contented.

I received great pain from being informed, that you are distressed on my account. Be of good cheer, I pray you. . . . It gives me pain, that I am separated from those I love, but comparing this with what thousands suffer, I dare not. . . . I would that it were in my power to solace and comfort your declining age. . . . And now, my dear madam, let me again entreat you to make yourself happy. Discard the gloomy ideas, which are too apt to crowd into the mind in your situation and time of life. There is enough of sorrow in this world, without looking into futurity for it. Hope the best. If it happens, well; if not, it will then be time enough to be afflicted, and at any rate the intermediate space will be well filled. Adieu.

Yours, most affectionately,

Gouverneur Morris.[2]

Throughout the long years of war, Morris had not seen his mother, Sarah Gouverneur Morris. Only two of his letters to her from that period survive. This one, written April 17, 1778, displays an affectionate side of Morris seldom displayed in public.

Morrisania for Sale

On January 15, 1786, Sarah Gouverneur died at the age of seventy-one. Richard Morris was the executor of her estate, meaning that he was chosen to execute the terms of her will. Soon after Sarah's death, Richard Morris advertised that all the family slaves would be sold—not freed—on April 12 of that year.[3]

But what would happen to Morrisania? After all, the property was one of the greatest land estates of all New York. It held both commercial and sentimental value to the family. Lewis Morris III had received his share of the estate. He was not interested in purchasing Morrisania. Richard Morris indicated that he was not interested in the property, either. The opportunity fell to Gouverneur Morris, who went through nearly six months of negotiations. Morris became exasperated with the length of the proceedings. In March 1787, he wrote his friend that:

> I am not so attached to that Purchase as to walk towards it on bad Ground. My Title to the Premises devised must be perfect and if all others act with the same good faith that I do there can be no Difficulty about the Matter.[4]

The agreement was finally made on April 4, 1787. Morris received the nineteen-hundred-acre estate, which had belonged to the family for

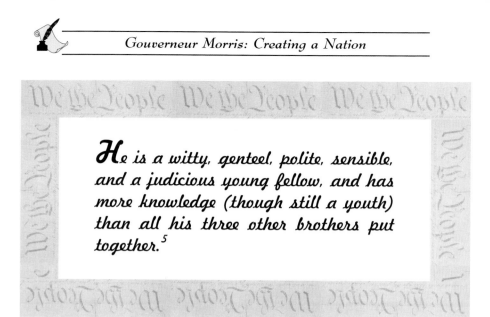

He is a witty, genteel, polite, sensible, and a judicious young fellow, and has more knowledge (though still a youth) than all his three other brothers put together.[5]

Judge Thomas Jones, known as a keen judge of character, had been chief justice of the supreme court of the New York colony before the American Revolution. In 1776, he remarked that Gouverneur Morris was a more intelligent young man than his brothers. This intelligence would help Morris as he negotiated the purchase of Morrisania.

more than one hundred years. Things had come full circle in the life of Gouverneur Morris.

Shays's Rebellion

While he was engaged in the negotiations for the family estate, Morris was elected to attend the Constitutional Convention as a delegate for Pennsylvania—not New York. These delegates were to meet in Philadelphia in May 1787.[6]

The Articles of Confederation had governed the thirteen states since 1781. Under the Articles, each of the thirteen states was basically sovereign, or free to self-govern. The Congress of the

Confederation could not take taxes or soldiers from the individual states. It could only make requests. The events of Shays's Rebellion in the summer and fall of 1786 showed the weakness of this type of government.

Daniel Shays was a farmer from Pelham, Massachusetts. He served throughout the American Revolution and became a captain. He returned home and found himself and many of his fellow farmers in debt. Shays's organized a resistance that included closing courthouses. His followers stood in front of courthouses and displayed their muskets. This prevented judges and juries from holding session. Shays and his followers were defeated by a large militia sent from Boston toward the end of 1786.

Although the rebellion was suppressed, commentators such as Alexander Hamilton and George Washington were now convinced that a stronger form of government was needed. Morris and his fellow delegates began to arrive at Philadelphia toward the end of May 1787 in order to create a new government for the United States.

Large and Small, Rich and Poor

THE CONSTITUTIONAL Convention met on Monday, May 14, 1787. The delegates gathered at the State House in Philadelphia, but agreed to wait until more members arrived. On Friday, May 25, enough delegates had arrived for the convention to begin. Morris was one of seven delegates from Pennsylvania. The others were Robert Morris, Thomas FitzSimons, James Wilson, George Clymer, Thomas Mifflin, and Jared Ingersoll. They were later joined by another delegate, Benjamin Franklin.

On the first day of the proceedings, Robert Morris moved that a president of the convention

Doubts About America's Future

Many people, both in America and Europe, doubted that the United States could endure as a nation. The United States stretched from Maine in the north to Georgia in the south. Skeptics pointed out that no democracy had ever been established in such a large land area. Skeptics declared that the only successful republics were located in small land areas—the Netherlands, Switzerland, and Venice.

be elected by ballot. Morris's respected friend, George Washington, was unanimously chosen.

Monday, May 28, was the second day of the convention. Rules were proposed for how the convention would operate. The delegates agreed that at least seven states must be represented on each day of business. If there were fewer than seven, the convention would not meet. It was agreed that each member would address George Washington when rising to speak. As a member spoke, no one should speak, whisper, pass notes, or even read any other material.[1] Also, no member should speak more than twice on the same question or motion. On the next day, other rules were presented. These were some of the most important:

1. No copies of any documents were allowed outside the State House.

2. Only members of the convention were allowed to read the official journal of the proceedings.

3. The conversations and debates within the State House were to remain private, not to be shared outside the building.[2]

The convention would conduct its business in private. The public would not be informed of the progress or the difficulties that occurred inside the closed doors of the State House. Most members of the convention believed this secrecy was necessary, but there were critics. From overseas in Paris, Thomas Jefferson commented that the secret tone of the convention cast suspicion upon its members and their decisions.

The Virginia Plan

On Tuesday, May 29, 1787, Virginia delegate Edmund Randolph made a series of proposals to the convention.[3] Randolph's proposals have become known as the Virginia Plan, or the Larger States' Plan. Randolph wanted a new governing body made up of two houses. He went on to propose that the people of the each state would elect the members of the first house. The members of the second house would be elected by the members of the first. Randolph called for a "National Executive," who would be chosen by the two houses and serve a term of a fixed number of years.

Randolph's plan appealed to states with large populations, such as Virginia and New York. It did not appeal to those with small populations, like Rhode Island and Delaware. Under the Virginia Plan, the small states would end up with fewer representatives in the legislature.

Debate over the Virginia Plan began on Wednesday. That day, Gouverneur Morris made his first statements to the convention. Morris made a "friendly amendment" to Randolph's plan:

> Resolved that a union of the States, merely federal, will not accomplish the objects proposed by the articles of confederation, namely "common defence, security of liberty, and general welfare."[4]

Immediately, questions were raised on the convention floor. What was a *federal* government compared to a *national* government? Morris explained the difference. A federal government was merely a treaty between the different states. The second government had complete powers. When pressed about why a national government was needed, Morris replied: "We had better take a supreme government now, than a despot [tyrant] twenty years hence—for come he must."[5]

Edmund Randolph was Virginia's delegate to the Constitutional Convention in 1787. He proposed the Virginia Plan, or the Larger States' Plan.

Morris had defined beliefs about government, even though he was younger than many other members of the convention. He believed that any type of loose government, which relied on voluntary agreement, would be insufficient. According to Morris, people would eventually want something that was stronger, and what they would receive would be a dictator.

Morris left the convention and departed for Morrisania the very next day. Morris had hired a group of workers and an overseer to manage his estate.[6] He wanted to make sure the work was being done to his satisfaction. Morris returned to Philadelphia and the convention floor on Monday, July 2.[7]

During Morris's month of absence, the Constitutional Convention had moved slowly forward. It had been decided that the delegates intended to create a national government, but what form it was to take remained very much up in the air. The large states continued to favor the plan put forward by Virginian Edmund Randolph. The smaller states favored a plan proposed by delegate William Patterson of New Jersey. Patterson proposed the creation of a government composed of the exact same number of men from each state, rather than on the basis of population. This would ensure that states like New Jersey and Georgia would always have the same number of representatives as larger states.

On July 2, delegate Roger Sherman of Connecticut commented that the convention was in a most dire moment: "We are now at a full stop, and nobody he supposed meant that we shd. [should] break up without doing

Morris's Absence

Today, it seems incredible that Morris would leave the Constitutional Convention for a whole month. His leave of absence demonstrates that, in the eighteenth century, most politicians were "part-time." This means that they were expected to support themselves financially from other occupations.

Morris had great wealth within the estate of Morrisania, but it required much of his attention. He went back to his land whenever his presence was required.

something."[8] Immediately after Sherman made this observation, Morris made one of his longest and most important speeches.

In his speech, Morris suggested creating an upper house of men selected by the president for life terms. Some delegates accused Morris of trying to set up an aristocracy because the upper house would be appointed for life and the lower house elected for terms of service. In other words, the lower house, selected by the American people, would serve a term of a specific number of years. At the same time, the upper house, selected by the upper class, would be in office for life.

In response to critics accusing him of serving the interest of the rich, Morris answered:

> The Rich will strive to establish their dominion & enslave the rest. They always did. They always will. The proper security agst [against] them is to form them into a separate interest. . . . By thus combining & setting apart, the aristocratic interest, the popular interest will be combined agst. [against] it. There will be a mutual check and security.[9]

To Morris, the issue was clear. Society consisted of the struggle between the rich and poor. Government was intended to protect private property and to prevent class warfare. Therefore, let government obviously separate the poor and

The Roman Republic

Though he did not explicitly say so, Morris's separation of the upper house and lower house may have come from the history of the Roman Republic.

From about 500 B.C. until the time of Julius Caesar, the Roman Republic was divided between a senate and a group of tribunes. The Senate was composed of aristocrats, while the tribunes were elected by the lower class. The senators and tribunes checked and balanced one another.

Morris believed that an upper house appointed for life and a lower house elected for terms of service would do the same in America.

Until the time of Julius Caesar (pictured), a senate and tribunes governed the Roman Republic.

the rich. Let the two groups watch over one another.

Even many delegates who agreed with Morris's ideas were offended by his blunt language. Was Roger Sherman right? Was the convention at a full stop? Or could the convention move forward to create a new government?

Free or Slave, President or King?

JUST ONE DAY AFTER the "full stop," the Constitutional Convention resolved an important issue. It was decided that the upper house of the legislature would have an equal number of representatives for each state.

With that settled, the convention moved to another, equally difficult topic. How should African Americans—whether they were slaves or free—be represented in the new government?

A proposal was made that African-American slaves should be counted as 3/5 of a person for the purpose of representation. This meant that states with large slave populations, such as

Virginia and North Carolina, would have a larger total population even though African-American slaves had no voice in the government. Because a state's number of representatives to the lower house was based on its population, slave states would have more representatives in the lower house. Many northern states still had slaves, but the numbers were small enough that they would not increase the number of representatives.

Speaking Against Slavery

Morris showed a noble side of his character at this point. One might think he would be comfortable with the institution of slavery because he had grown up at Morrisania, where his father owned over fifty slaves. Instead, Morris was against slavery. On August 8, 1787, he rose to speak his mind on the subject:

> Mr. Gov. Morris moved to insert 'free' before the word 'inhabitants.' Much he said would depend on this point. He never would concur [agree] in upholding domestic slavery. It was a nefarious [immoral] institution—It was the curse of heaven on the States where it prevailed. Compare the free regions of the Middle States, where a rich & noble cultivation marks the prosperity & happiness of the people, with the misery & poverty which overspreads the barren wastes of Va. Maryd. & the other States having slaves.[1]

During the 1787 Constitutional Convention, delegates addressed how African Americans would be represented in the new government.

Morris felt that slavery should be abolished altogether. His speech used the differences between the northern, middle, and southern states to demonstrate the negative impact of the slave system.

Although he had already said much that might offend his southern colleagues, Morris also criticized the way African-American slaves were counted in the overall population of a state. This gave a state more representatives and power in the lower house, but did not give the African-American slaves any rights. He added:

> Upon what principle is it that the slaves shall be computed in the representation? Are they men? Then make them Citizens & let them vote? Are they property? Why then is no other property included?[2]

Morris was the first founding father to push the issue of abolition this far. He committed himself to the idea that a new government should free every African American. He was against the nation moving forward with a method of representation that neglected that African-American population's concerns. If his words were not as eloquent as those of later abolitionists John Brown or William Lloyd Garrison, remember that Morris spoke these words in 1787— approximately seventy-five years before Abraham Lincoln wrote the Emancipation Proclamation.

Morris detested slavery and became the first founding father to push for abolition.

Unfortunately, none of Morris's efforts succeeded. The Convention agreed to the principle of 3/5 representation for African-American slaves.

President or King?

Morris had another great contribution to

make. When it came to the creation of the executive branch—the branch of government that enforces the laws—there was much discussion in the Constitutional Convention. Should there be one executive or two? Should such a person be elected by the people or appointed? Should the term be for a fixed number of years or for life?

The question of presidential election came up on Tuesday, July 17, 1787. A resolution called for a single executive to be chosen by the upper and lower houses of the legislature. Morris rose at once to dispute the point:

> He [the executive] ought to be elected by the people at large, by the freeholders of the Country. . . . If the people should elect, they will never fail to prefer some man of distinguished character, or services . . .[3]

Morris spoke swiftly and to the point. He was the first to call for election by the people. But Morris's speech did not have its desired effect. The delegates turned down the idea of popular election of the executive by nine states to one. Only Pennsylvania voted in favor.

The resolution also proposed that the executive serve a term of seven years. The executive would be ineligible for a second term. When delegate William Houston of New Jersey moved to strike the ineligibility clause, Morris rose in

He finds that the Executive is not to be re-eligible. What effect will this have? 1. it will destroy the great incitement to merit public esteem by taking away the hope of being rewarded with a reappointment. It may give a dangerous turn to one of the strongest passions in the human breast. The love of fame is the great spring to noble & illustrious actions. Shut the Civil road to Glory & he may be compelled to seek it by the sword. 2. It will tempt him to make the most of the Short space of time allotted him, to accumulate wealth and provide for his friends. 3. It will produce violations of the very constitution it is meant to secure.[4]

On July 19, 1787, Morris delivered the longest speech that he ever gave before the Constitutional Convention. In it, he explored the possible consequences should the executive not be eligible for reelection.

agreement. He reasoned that taking away the opportunity to be reelected "tended to destroy the great motive to good behavior, the hope of being rewarded by a re-appointment."[5]

Six states voted in favor of striking the clause. Four were in favor of keeping it.

The discussion continued on Thursday, July 19, 1787. Later that same day the votes came. It was decided, by a vote of eight to two, that the executive could be eligible for reelection.

Treachery and Bribery

On Friday, July 20, 1787, the Constitutional Convention explored the matter of impeachment—the removal of an official from office. Morris was originally opposed to any form of impeachment. He believed the threat of being impeached would make the executive cater to the goals of the upper and lower houses because they could remove him from office if he acted against them. During the course of the debate, Morris changed his mind. He agreed that the executive could be impeached, but only for the crimes of treachery (treason) and bribery (taking a bribe).[6] The Convention voted in favor of impeachment by eight states to two.

By the beginning of September 1787, the Constitutional Convention had accomplished a lot of work. Morris and his fellow delegates had agreed upon a basic framework of government. Although Morris had not succeeded in winning many of his arguments, he was outspoken in his views against slavery and in favor of a powerful executive.

We the People

ON SATURDAY, SEPTEMBER 8, 1787, the Constitutional Convention appointed a Committee of Style to put the finishing touches on the document that was to become the U.S. Constitution. The committee consisted of five delegates: James Madison, William Samuel Johnson, Alexander Hamilton, Rufus King, and Gouverneur Morris.[1] Johnson was chairman of the committee, but most of the editing and polish given to the document came from Morris.

Editing Process

On Wednesday, September 12, the Committee of Style presented its draft of the Constitution.

The delegates sat back to listen to the revised document.

When the convention had originally handed the document to the Committee of Style, the Constitution began with these words:

> We the People of the States of New-Hampshire, Massachusetts, Rhode-Island and Providence Plantations, Connecticut, New-York, New-Jersey, Pennsylvania, Delaware, Maryland, Virginia, North-Carolina, South-Carolina, and Georgia, do ordain, declare and establish the following Constitution for the Government of Ourselves and our Posterity.[2]

This version listed the thirteen different states by name. It implied that the states were coming together to create this Constitution, and this new nation. When the Committee of Style read its revised version, the document began:

> We the People of the United States, in Order to form a more perfect Union, to establish Justice, insure domestic Tranquility, provide for the common Defence, promote the general Welfare, and secure the Blessings of Liberty to ourselves and our Posterity, do ordain and establish this Constitution for the United States of America.[3]

What a difference between the first and second versions! The new version struck out the names of the states, and declared simply, "We the People." Sometimes the power of words is overlooked. Morris and the other members of the Committee of Style may simply have wanted the document to be more straightforward. But the results of this editorial change were profound.

For the next seventy-five years, American statesmen and orators would argue over the meaning of the Constitution. Was it an agreement made among the thirteen states? Or among the American people? If the agreement was among the states, then individual states should be able to depart from the United States when they chose. If the agreement was among the American people, then no state had the right to leave the Union.

Morris leaned toward firm nationalism. The words "We the People" served those, like him, who interpreted the Constitution as an agreement among the people rather than among the states.

There was another significant change, as well. What had been a document of twenty-three articles now contained only seven. Article I dealt with the legislative branch, Article II with the executive branch, and Article III handled the judicial power of the United States. Article IV discussed the relationship between states, as well as the possibility of admitting new ones. Article V explored the process of creating amendments to the Constitution if necessary. The distinction between federal and state law was discussed within Article VI. Finally, Article VII explained the process of ratifying the Constitution.

Morris and his fellow committee members had completed an immense undertaking. They had put the Constitutional Convention's resolutions for a new government into words. Following the presentation of their revision came a final round of debates.

Delegates Divided

Delegates Edmund Randolph, Elbridge Gerry of Massachusetts, and George Mason of Virginia were opposed to the revised Constitution. On Saturday, September 15, 1787, the men took the floor and presented their arguments against the document.

Edmund Randolph spoke first. He felt that the revised version of the Constitution gave too much power to the legislative branch. Like many Virginians, Randolph believed that a weak federal government was preferable to a powerful one. The great Virginian orator Patrick Henry had declined to even come to the Constitutional Convention, convinced that the government would be too strong.

George Mason spoke next. Like Randolph, Mason believed that, in its new form, the Constitution gave too much power to the federal government.

Last, Elbridge Gerry presented his arguments against the Constitution. He was specific in his

Gerrymander

Elbridge Gerry

Constitutional Convention delegate Elbridge Gerry later served as governor of Massachusetts. While governor, Gerry led the way in redrawing voting districts in Massachusetts. During this process, one of the new districts on the map of Massachusetts looked like a salamander. One person quickly called it a "gerrymander." The name stuck. Today, when districts are redrawn to benefit one political party, we still call them gerrymanders, or say they have been gerrymandered.

list of objections to the new revised version of the document. Gerry had a total of eleven objections—eight of which he admitted were small matters. But there were three items he found impossible to accept:

1. That the legislative branch would have the power to create whatever laws it pleased;
2. That the new government would be able to raise money without limit, and therefore could maintain a standing army; and
3. That the government could establish a new court system that would be independent of any form of review.

For these reasons, Gerry refused to sign.[4]

The delegates took Sunday off. On Monday, September 17, they returned to the State House to accept or reject the Constitution.

On this day, Benjamin Franklin took the floor to give his view on the document. Franklin was the oldest, most distinguished delegate. In terms of popularity and admiration, he was second only to George Washington. Franklin, who had long ago made his name and money through the publication of *Poor Richard's Almanac*, knew a decisive moment when he saw one. Franklin delivered a reasoned, but passionate, speech in favor of accepting the Constitution. Franklin urged all the delegates to show unity and sign the document.

During the Constitutional Convention, Benjamin Franklin urged all the delegates to show unity by signing the new Constitution.

Benjamin Franklin's wish was not fulfilled. Randolph announced his unwillingness to sign. Gerry and Mason also announced that they would not sign the document. In response, Morris declared that he, too, had doubts, but considered this Constitution to be the best choice.

Even though not every delegate stood

The Federalist

The delegates of the Constitutional Convention had written the Constitution, but it had to be ratified by nine of the thirteen states in order to become law. Gouverneur Morris played little part in the ratification process, but his friends John Jay and Alexander Hamilton played a large role.

Together with James Madison, they wrote a series of anonymous essays to newspapers in New York City, hoping to persuade people to vote in favor of ratification. The collected essays, written in 1787 and 1788, were called *The Federalist*.

In these essays, Jay, Hamilton, and Madison pointed out the need for a stronger central government. They viewed the Constitution as the best document that could be agreed upon. They emphasized that the checks and balances system of the Constitution would create a strong government and still guard states' rights.

Alexander Hamilton

James Madison

behind the new Constitution, the signing took place. The delegates arranged themselves by groups according to the states that they represented. The groups began with New Hampshire and concluded with Georgia. Morris was near the middle of the group.

While the last members were signing the parchment document, Benjamin Franklin remarked to delegate James Madison that he was pleased to see the convention had succeeded in finishing its work.

Their work was over. The delegates went home the next day. Among them, they had created the document that became the U.S. Constitution. The delegates of thirteen states had helped create a new nation.

After the Constitutional Convention, Morris returned to private life. He was not involved in the effort during the next twelve months to persuade individual states to ratify the new Constitution. Instead, Morris was actively engaged in business interests.

In the autumn of 1788, Morris agreed to travel to France to pursue the interests of a firm that exported tobacco from Virginia. Little did Morris know that he would be away from the United States for the next ten years.

American Abroad

GOUVERNEUR MORRIS ARRIVED in Paris, France, in January 1789.[1] His passage across the Atlantic, during a cold, harsh winter, had taken forty days. Morris arrived at a time when the French government and society were on the verge of revolution.

French society was organized into three classes, or estates. The First Estate was the clergy. The Second Estate was the nobility. The Third Estate was the middle class, which was growing steadily in number. For hundreds of years, the clergy and nobility had been exempt from paying tax in France.

King Louis XVI and Queen Marie Antoinette had spent great sums of money assisting the American states in their struggle for independence. France had done this in order to weaken England, but it now appeared that the French economy had suffered more than that of the British.

The combination of the tax exemption of the clergy and nobles along with the expenses of the American Revolution brought France to bankruptcy. In 1789, representatives of the Three Estates met at Versailles, the royal palace, to discuss how best to handle the situation. The situation was volatile, because prices were rising every day.

Morris might have stayed out of the entire matter. He was only a businessman. But, because of his friendship with the Marquis de Lafayette, Morris was able to move with ease in French society. Morris had first met the Marquis de Lafayette in America in 1777. Through the Frenchman, Morris was introduced to both the king and queen. He was also able to observe the opening of the new French legislature—the Estates General—in May 1789.

The volatile situation burst in the summer of 1789. In June, the delegates of the Three Estates announced that they would meet together rather than separately, as had always been the custom.

They renamed themselves the National Assembly. This political upheaval was followed by a violent rebellion on July 14, known today as Bastille Day. On this day, Parisian crowds obtained guns, pitchforks, and knives. They converged on the Bastille, an ancient fortress where political prisoners were held. The crowd forced open the Bastille, killed its governor, and placed his head on a spike. Only seven prisoners were found and released. Morris was horrified by these events. When he learned that the Bastille had fallen, Morris described:

France's Queen Marie Antoinette (left) and King Louis XVI (right) spent large amounts of money during the American Revolution. This hurt their nation's economy.

Houdon's Statue

French sculptor Jean-Antoine Houdon (1741–1828) was one of the best-known artists of the 1700s, both in his homeland and across the ocean in the United States.

After the American Revolution, Houdon was commissioned to create a statue of America's George Washington. The sculptor needed someone to pose for this marble statue. Houdon approached Gouverneur Morris for this purpose. Morris and Washington were about the same height, although Morris was portlier.

On June 5, 1789, Morris wrote in his diary: "I stand for his statue of General Washington, being the humble employment of a manikin [mannequin]."[2] The statue was a great success. Today, it stands in the Virginia State Capitol in Richmond.

The Washington Statue

> While sitting here, a person comes and announces the taking of the Bastile, the Governor of which is beheaded . . . They are carrying the heads in triumph through the city. The carrying of this citadel is among the most extraordinary things, that I have met with. It cost the assailants sixty men, it is said.[3]

The National Assembly then took their revolt farther. That summer, the delegates of the

National Assembly—the Marquis de Lafayette among them—abolished the ancient system of feudal rights and privileges. Feudalism was a system in which a figurehead, like a king, rules over aristocrats and peasants alike. Morris did not approve of abolishing this system in France. He believed that the French were not ready for self-government.

In January 1790, Morris received two letters from George Washington. Morris's friend and

In 1789, Parisian crowds used weapons and violence to force open the Bastille, a fortress where political prisoners were kept.

colleague had been elected as the first president of the United States. Washington had been inaugurated in April 1789. President Washington now asked Morris to go to London as an informal ambassador. Washington asked Morris to persuade the British to evacuate their forts in the "Old Northwest" area. Today, this area is Indiana, Illinois, and Ohio.[4]

During this same time, Morris knew that a major diplomatic conflict was brewing between England and Spain. Knowing that France and Spain usually worked together against England, Morris tried to convince some Frenchmen to begin a war with England. By doing so, Morris argued, the French would close ranks behind their King Louis XVI. This would prevent the type of revolutionary chaos that Morris foresaw happening in France.

Morris then left for England. He met with the Duke of Leeds, who was foreign secretary of the British government. Morris was not one bit uncomfortable with the British aristocracy. Morris conducted himself with skill, but he failed to make the British budge from the Old Northwest. He was also unable to bring about a war between England and the alliance of France and Spain.

The failure was not due to lack of effort. In June 1790, Morris wrote a long memorandum for

In 1789, crowds gathered in New York to watch George Washington (on the balcony) be inaugurated as the first president of the United States.

the Marquis de Lafayette. In it, Morris developed his ideas for a war strategy. Morris even planned for a French invasion of England. Morris's document ended with words of high hopes. Morris envisioned a new world order, in which the British were reduced and a balance of power established on the European continent.[5] As outrageous as Morris's maneuvering seemed, points and predictions in the memorandum came true in time.

Eventually, Morris returned to France. Throughout 1791, he witnessed the French revolutionaries become more and more radical. Morris may have been frustrated by the events, but he was now offered a new opportunity to work on the situation. On April 6, 1792, he learned that he had been appointed the new American ambassador to France.

President Washington congratulated Morris on the appointment, but also warned him that many voices had been raised against him in the U.S. Senate. Prominent American senators claimed Morris was too loud, too imaginative, and too decisive. President Washington urged Morris to be more careful and cautious in his new position as American ambassador.[6] Meanwhile, the French Revolution had reached a new level of violence.

The Reign of Terror

In August 1792, King Louis XVI and Queen Marie Antoinette were arrested

In 1790, the Marquis de Lafayette received a memorandum from Morris with ideas for a French invasion of England.

and placed in prison. King Louis XVI was found guilty of crimes against the French people. He was beheaded by the guillotine in January 1793. Queen Marie Antoinette followed a few months later.[7]

Now, some of Morris's predictions began to come true. England and Spain soon went to war with France. The British and Spanish were horrified at the execution of King Louis XVI and Queen Marie Antoinette. Austria and Prussia entered the war as allies of the British and Spanish. French revolutionaries faced four powerful enemies. As the allied armies won victories, the people in Paris became increasingly upset and desperate.

Suspecting that there were traitors among them, the Parisians began to accuse many people of the charge of being a "counterrevolutionary." This meant simply being against the French Revolution. Charges were made. People were arrested and given speedy trials. Daily, one heard the beating of drums, the roll of cartwheels, and the sharp hiss as the blade of the guillotine descended on the heads of the unfortunate counterrevolutionaries. This period was known as the Reign of Terror.

Thousands of people died during the Reign of Terror. Throughout this time, Morris remained in his political post as ambassador to France. He

In August 1792, King Louis XVI was arrested and thrown into prison. Here, he is pictured with his family the night before his execution.

lent money to French aristocrats seeking to escape France and hid others in his apartments. He could not rescue his friend the Marquis de Lafayette. As the violence became more extreme, aristocrat Marquis de Lafayette became a fugitive and was thrown into an Austrian prison. Try as he might, Morris could not free his friend at this time because the United States had little influence with the Austrian government. Morris was, however, able to help save Lafayette's wife and children from poverty and starvation by financially supporting them.

In July 1794, Maximilien Robespierre, leader of the most radical French faction, was arrested

In their eagerness to abolish ancient institutions they forgot that a monarchy without intermediate ranks is but another name for anarchy or despotism.[8]

In 1792, just six months before the Reign of Terror began, Morris wrote a letter to statesman Thomas Jefferson, who was in America. In the letter, Morris criticized the French for overthrowing their king without having a replacing government designed.

The Guillotine

Until the 1790s, most executions in France were performed by a headsman who used an axe. The guillotine, invented in the 1780s, changed the preferred method of execution. By operating this device, a sharp blade came whistling down a distance of twenty feet. The guillotine usually succeeded in decapitating a person with one try. It was meant to be a humane instrument, because the headsman's axe often took two or three tries to complete the beheading. But the guillotine made executions quicker and easier with its marvelous efficiency.

The guillotine

and guillotined. Morris was recalled to the United States after the French government requested his dismissal. James Monroe, who had opposed Morris's original appointment, arrived in August 1794 as a replacement.[9]

Morris could have returned home right away, but he had developed a taste for travel. He stayed in France until October, then traveled through Switzerland and Germany for the next eight months. In June 1795, he went to London, England, where he remained for the next year.

Morris had initially believed that the French, under King Louis XVI, would be America's best ally. But now, with the king dead and France still in unrest, Morris had become a firm believer in the British system of government and an American friendship with England.

After leaving London, Morris moved on to the countries of Switzerland, Austria, and Germany. He circulated among the highest social groups. Not until October 1798 did Morris sail for home. He landed in New York on December 23, having been away from home for almost exactly ten years.

Last Years

IN DECEMBER 1798, Morris came home to a nation that had undergone significant changes. When he had left in December 1788, George Washington had not yet been inaugurated as the first president. There had also been no political parties.

Now, on his return, Morris found John Adams leading the Federalist Party. This party favored a strong central government, which placed the interests of commerce and manufacturing over the interests of agriculture. Morris was a Federalist. He had always believed in strong government with an informal aristocracy playing a large role in it.

Morris opposed the political views of Thomas Jefferson, leader of the new Democratic-Republican Party. This party believed that the U.S. Constitution had to be strictly interpreted. It also claimed that the states and people should retain as many of their powers and rights as possible. Always ready to fight for what he believed in, Morris was ready to enter politics once more.

Death of a Hero

George Washington died on December 14, 1799. The entire country mourned, including Morris. Because of his reputation for speech making and friendship with Washington, Morris was asked to give the eulogy, a speech that recalls and praises an individual who has passed away. Morris did so, enlarging his own reputation in the process.

Morris was elected to the U.S. Senate in April 1800. During the Constitutional Convention, he had believed that members

Thomas Jefferson was the leader of the Democratic-Republican Party.

should be appointed for life. As it turned out, Morris would enjoy three years filling out the term of James Watson, who had resigned.[1]

There were no popular votes cast in 1800. Americans did not begin casting popular votes—the votes of the people—until 1824. Every presidential election between 1789 and 1824 was decided through the votes of the Electoral College—a group of representatives chosen by the voters of each state to elect the president and vice president. When the votes were counted at the beginning of 1801, Thomas Jefferson held the lead, but no one had obtained a majority number of votes. The result was that the election was "thrown" into the House of Representatives—the lower house of the legislative branch. Members of the House of Representatives, unlike the Senate and the presidency, were elected by popular votes. They would now decide who would become president.

Statesman Alexander Hamilton urged the electors who supported him to cast their votes for opponent Thomas Jefferson. Hamilton feared that Aaron Burr, whom he considered unscrupulous, might win. Because of this plotting, Jefferson was elected president. As the candidate with the next largest number of votes, Burr received the vice-presidency. This was the method of choosing the vice president during this time.

Gouverneur Morris had no chance to vote in the runoff that elected Thomas Jefferson because Morris was a member of the Senate, not the House of Representatives. But Morris had many opportunities to witness the bickering that followed, and it must be confessed that he played some part in it.

Morris and Jefferson had never been close. In 1789 when Morris visited Jefferson in Paris, both men had commented on their inability to see

Alexander Hamilton (left) believed that statesman Aaron Burr (right) was an unscrupulous man.

things in the same light. Now, as Jefferson become the third president of the United States, Morris had the opportunity to strike out against one of his fellow founding fathers.

Political Squabbles

Morris had long been suspicious of states in the western United States. During Constitutional debates, he had argued against making those areas into states. Morris claimed doing this would lead the country into a war with Spain. Now, it seemed likely that the western states would lead the country into a war with France.

Napoleon Bonaparte, who had become the first consul of France in 1800, was ambitious for a new French empire in North America. He had secretly forced Spain to return the Louisiana area to France. President Jefferson saw the French control of Louisiana as a direct threat to the United States. He initiated negotiations to purchase the land from France.

Morris spoke out against President Jefferson's negotiations with France. As late as 1803, when the Louisiana Purchase was being completed between American negotiators and French diplomats in France, Morris spoke out against Jefferson and his policies.[2]

In 1803, Morris left the Senate. He did not participate in the Senate debates over the

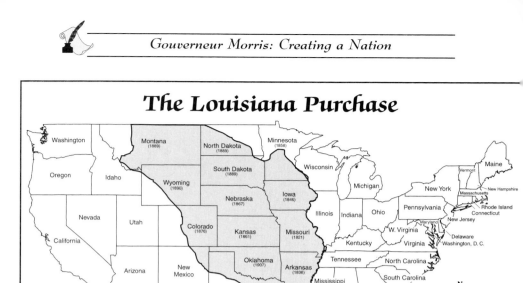

The Louisiana Purchase

States of the Louisiana Purchase

This map shows the territory gained from the Louisiana Purchase. Gouverneur Morris was opposed to this deal.

Louisiana Purchase. Morris was a private citizen at last.

In the summer of 1804, a personal feud led to a political crisis. Aaron Burr and Alexander Hamilton had never forgiven one another for the roles they had played in the election of 1800. Now, Burr claimed that Hamilton had spread slanderous charges about his character. Burr challenged Hamilton to a duel.

The two men met at Weehawken Heights, New Jersey, on the morning of July 11, 1804. Last minute attempts to bring about reconciliation

Dueling

Dueling is a form of combat between two armed persons, which is carried out according to set rules. In the past, a person who believed that he had been insulted could challenge an offender. The man challenged had his choice of weapons. Duelists would usually use swords or pistols. The two men who fought the duel were called the *principals*. Each principal chose a friend, who was called his *second*. Sometimes an accident happened to a principal, and his second had to stand in for him.

Some duels were fatal; others were not. In the 1800s, French duelists were content with inflicting wounds. Most Americans, on the other hand, demanded death. This form of settling disputes was a common feature of early American society.

Aaron Burr's shot at Alexander Hamilton is one of history's most famous examples of a fatal duel.

failed, and the duel proceeded as a matter of honor. According to the rules of the time, the two men marched ten paces, then turned and were free to fire. Hamilton fired his pistol into the air as a way of showing he bore Burr no malice. But Burr leveled his pistol and shot a bullet that pierced Hamilton's chest.[3]

Hamilton was brought to his home, where he died the next day. Burr, although he was the vice president, would eventually be indicted for murder in New York and New Jersey. Hamilton's funeral was scheduled for July 14. Morris was asked to deliver the funeral oration for Alexander Hamilton. As an old friend of Hamilton, Morris naturally accepted.[4]

The funeral was one of the largest events in the history of New York City. The funeral procession went to Trinity Church. On a stage that had been erected, Gouverneur Morris stood beside four of Alexander Hamilton's sons and delivered the eulogy.

In May 1806, Robert Morris died in Philadelphia. The great financier had fallen on very hard times. He had spent several years in debtors' jail and had emerged from the ordeal penniless. It was a sad end to the man who—along with Gouverneur Morris—had piloted the finances of the United States between 1781 and 1784.

Students of Columbia—he was in the ardent pursuit of knowledge in your academic shades, when the first sound of the American war called him to the field. A young and unprotected volunteer, such was his zeal, and so brilliant his service, that we herald his name before we knew his person. It seemed as if God had called him suddenly into existence, that he might assist to save a world! . . .

Fellow Citizens—You have long witnessed his professional conduct, and felt his unrivaled eloquence. You know how well he performed the duties of a Citizen—you know that he never courted your favour by adulation, or the sacrifice of his own judgment. . . . I CHARGE YOU TO PROTECT HIS FAME—It is all he has left—all that these poor orphan children will inherit from his father. But, my countrymen, that Fame may be a rich treasure to you also. Let it be the test by which to examine those who solicit your favour. Disregarding professions, view their conduct and on a doubtful occasion, ask, Would Hamilton have done this thing?[5]

Gouverneur Morris delivered an eloquent tribute to his friend and fellow founding father, Alexander Hamilton. In the speech, Morris praised the lifetime achievements of Hamilton.

Robert Morris's will made a number of small bequests. The only one made to a nonfamily member was to Gouverneur Morris. Even at the end of his life, Robert Morris remembered Gouverneur. He left his friend: "my Telescope & espying glass."[6]

Marriage

On December 25, 1809, Morris married Nancy Randolph, his housekeeper. She was a member of a famous Virginia family and a descendant of Pocahontas, the daughter of an American Indian chief.

Morris had first met Nancy Randolph when he visited Virginia in 1788. Since that time, she had suffered personal tragedy. Randolph was accused of killing her baby and tried in 1794. Defended by Patrick Henry and John Marshall, Randolph was acquitted, or found not guilty. Her family still refused to have any contact with her, however. She moved to Connecticut, where she reunited with Morris. Morris later brought her to Morrisania, first as his housekeeper and then as his wife.[7]

Many of Morris's friends could scarcely believe he had finally married. They questioned Morris's rationale for marrying a woman who had little money. With typical sauciness, he commented to those who disapproved of his new wife:

> If I had married a rich Woman of seventy, the World might think it wiser than to take one of half that Age without a Farthing, and if the World were to live with my Wife I should certainly have consulted its Taste—but as that happens not to be the Case, I thought I might without offending others endeavor to suit myself, and look rather into the Head and Heart than into the Pocket.[8]

Morris had found a loving partner in Nancy Randolph. The couple had a son in 1813. They named him Gouverneur, Jr.[9]

The War of 1812

Morris was called back to public service in 1810. He was appointed chairman of a group of seven commissioners examining the possibility of a canal between the Hudson River and Lake Erie. Morris was a natural for the post because of his many contacts in the business world and the great deal of money he had invested in land in upstate New York. But the start of the War of 1812 put aside any plans for the canal.

When James Madison became president of the United States in 1809, the nation was facing several conflicts with England. Trade with Britain was one of the government's biggest problems. British warships had a pattern of interfering with American shipping. Reports that the British were provoking American Indians to attack Americans in the western United States also incited bad feelings against England. On top of this, a strongly nationalistic generation—known as "war hawks"—had appeared in politics. Madison knew the United States was unprepared for war, but he still asked for Congress's approval.

The War of 1812 was a great disappointment to Morris. Although Morris and Madison had worked closely together editing the U.S. Constitution, the pair held two different viewpoints on policy matters. Morris remained a Federalist, while Madison was a Democratic-Republican. Federalists who opposed Madison's decision for war, like Morris, referred to the War of 1812 as "Mr. Madison's War." It was painful for Morris to see the Democratic-Republican Party running the nation.

Final Days

The War of 1812 ended in 1815. Throughout the next year, Morris often talked about his oncoming death. He passed away on his estate at Morrisania on November 6, 1816, in the very room where he had been born.

Morris and many other founding fathers had left the stage. He was among the last of the great

> *Oh my adored, my best of husbands, had I been told this was to be the last morning we should leave our chamber together—that the last night we should reenter it together—I should have thought my heart would burst.*
>
> *. . . The precious remains of this wise and virtuous man are preserved in three coffins. The first having been made without a leaden lining. I trust in God I shall be laid close by this kindest of friends, this tenderly beloved husband.*[10]

Evidence of Nancy Randolph's love for her husband, Gouverneur Morris, is contained in this letter she wrote when learning of his death.

northern leaders of the Constitutional Convention. Today, Gouverneur Morris is buried at St. Ann's, an Episcopal church built by his son in 1841. This church is a small remnant of the grand estate that the Morris family once owned.

During his lifetime, Morris participated in the American Revolution, the Constitutional

Gouverneur Morris is buried at St. Ann's, a church in the Bronx.

Convention, and the writing of the U.S. Constitution. Later, he partook in the French Revolution and the early politics of the United States. Historian and future U.S. president Theodore Roosevelt, who wrote a biography of Morris in 1888, summed up the story of this founding father:

> There has never been an American statesman of keener intellect or more brilliant genius. . . . With all his faults, there are few men of his generation to whom the country owes more than to Gouverneur Morris.[11]

Throughout his career, Morris's essential beliefs did not change. He believed in freedom, and used his expert writing and speaking abilities to guarantee this freedom in America.

Timeline

1780
Fails to be reelected to Congress. Suffers the loss of a leg from an accident in Philadelphia.

1782
July 29: Presents the "Report on Public Credit" to Congress.

1752
January 31: Born at Morrisania in what is now the Bronx, New York.

1776
Heads a committee that examines the actions of known Loyalists.

1771
Licensed to practice law in New York.

1750　**1760**　**1770**　**1780**

1768
Graduates from King's College, New York.

1775
Elected to the Provincial Congress of New York. Is a member of the committee that welcomes General George Washington to New York City.

1781
July: Made assistant superintendent of finance for the United States, under Superintendent Robert Morris.

1777
Is a member of a committee that writes New York State's first constitution. Helps evacuate people from Kingston, the New York capital. Goes to Philadelphia as a member of the Second Continental Congress.

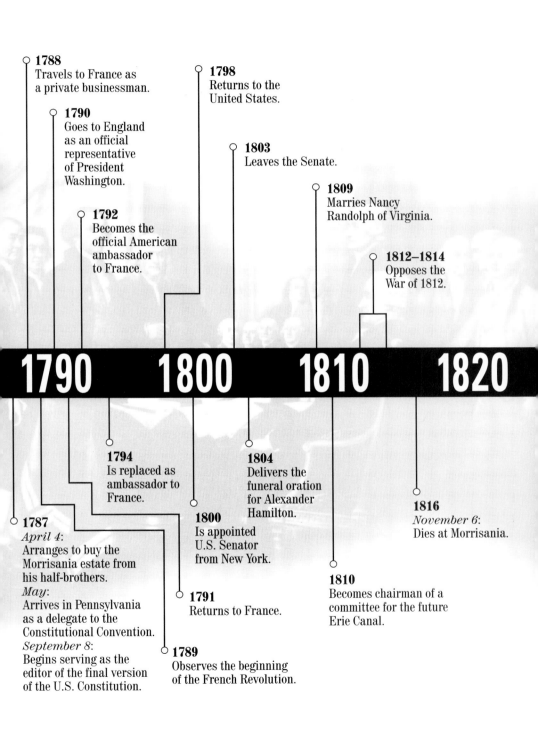

1788
Travels to France as a private businessman.

1790
Goes to England as an official representative of President Washington.

1792
Becomes the official American ambassador to France.

1798
Returns to the United States.

1803
Leaves the Senate.

1809
Marries Nancy Randolph of Virginia.

1812–1814
Opposes the War of 1812.

1790   1800   1810   1820

1794
Is replaced as ambassador to France.

1804
Delivers the funeral oration for Alexander Hamilton.

1816
November 6:
Dies at Morrisania.

1787
April 4:
Arranges to buy the Morrisania estate from his half-brothers.
May:
Arrives in Pennsylvania as a delegate to the Constitutional Convention.
September 8:
Begins serving as the editor of the final version of the U.S. Constitution.

1800
Is appointed U.S. Senator from New York.

1791
Returns to France.

1810
Becomes chairman of a committee for the future Erie Canal.

1789
Observes the beginning of the French Revolution.

Chapter Notes

Chapter 1. Year of the Hangman

1. John S. Bowman, ed., *Facts About the American Wars* (New York: H. W. Wilson, 1998), p. 81.

2. Max M. Mintz, *Gouverneur Morris and the American Revolution* (Norman: University of Oklahoma Press, 1970), pp. 79–80.

3. Jared Sparks, ed., *The Life of Gouverneur Morris, with Selections from His Correspondence and Miscellaneous Papers* (Boston: Gray & Brown, 1832), vol. 1, p. 132.

Chapter 2. Young Aristocrat

1. Eugene R. Sheridan, *Lewis Morris, 1671–1746: A Study in Early American Politics* (N.Y.: Syracuse University Press, 1981), pp. 9–10.

2. Ibid., p. 6.

3. Max M. Mintz, *Gouverneur Morris and the American Revolution* (Norman: University of Oklahoma Press, 1970), pp. 13–15.

4. Ibid., pp. 40–41.

5. Jared Sparks, ed., *The Life of Gouverneur Morris, with Selections from His Correspondence and Miscellaneous Papers* (Boston: Gray & Brown, 1832), vol. 1, p. 17.

6. Ibid., p. 25.

Chapter 3. New York Patriot

1. Martha J. Lamb, *History of the City of New York* (New York: A. S. Barnes & Co., 1877), p. 21.

2. Max M. Mintz, *Gouverneur Morris and the American Revolution* (Norman: University of Oklahoma Press, 1970), p. 46.

3. Ibid., p. 47.

4. Ibid., p. 48.

5. Malcolm Decker, *Brink of Revolution: New York in Crisis, 1765–1776* (New York: Argosy Antiquarian Ltd., 1964), pp. 197–200.

6. Mintz, pp. 69–70.

7. De Alva S. Alexander, *A Political History of the State of New York* (New York: Henry Holt and Company, 1906), p. 10.

8. Ibid., p. 9.

9. Ibid., pp. 9–13.

10. Mintz, p. 76.

11. Ibid., p. 85.

12. U.S. Congress, *Biographical Directory of the American Congress, 1774–1961* (Washington, D.C.: U.S. Government Printing Office, 1961), pp. 1359–1360.

Chapter 4. Morris and Morris

1. Max M. Mintz, *Gouverneur Morris and the American Revolution* (Norman: University of Oklahoma Press, 1970), p. 89.

2. Harlow Giles Unger, *Lafayette* (New York: John Wiley & Sons, Inc., 2002), p. 89.

3. Mintz, pp. 104–106.

4. Jared Sparks, ed., *The Life of Gouverneur Morris, with Selections from His Correspondence and Miscellaneous Papers* (Boston: Gray & Brown, 1832), vol. 1, pp. 215–216.

5. Ibid., p. 224.

6. Mintz, pp. 139–140.

7. Eleanor Young, *Forgotten Patriot, Robert Morris* (New York: Macmillan, 1950), p. 96.

8. Ibid., pp. 96–97.

9. Mintz, p. 148.

10. Ibid., pp. 151–152.

11. Ibid., p. 149.

12. Robert Morris, *The Papers of Robert Morris, 1781–1784*, E. James Ferguson, et al, eds. (Pa.: University of Pittsburgh Press, 1988), vol. 7, p. 271.

13. Mintz, pp. 155–156.

Chapter 5. Family Matters

1. Samuel Stelle Smith, *Lewis Morris, Anglo-American Statesman* (Atlantic Highlands, N.J.: Humanities Press Inc., 1983), pp. 95–96.

2. Jared Sparks, ed., *The Life of Gouverneur Morris, with Selections from His Correspondence and Miscellaneous Papers* (Boston: Gray & Brown, 1832), vol. 1, pp. 157–159.

3. Max M. Mintz, *Gouverneur Morris and the American Revolution* (Norman: University of Oklahoma Press, 1970), p. 172.

4. Ibid., p. 174.

5. Thomas Jones, *History of New York during the Revolutionary War, and of The Leading Events in the Other Colonies at that Period*, Edward Floyd de Lancey, ed. (New York: New York Historical Society, 1879), vol. 1, p. 140.

6. Mintz, p. 176.

Chapter 6. Large and Small, Rich and Poor

1. Max Farrand, ed., *The Records of the Federal Convention of 1787, four volumes* (New Haven, Conn.: Yale University Press, 1937), vol. 1, p. 8.

2. Ibid., p. 15.

3. Ibid., pp. 18–20.

4. Ibid., p. 30.

5. Ibid., p. 43.

6. Max M. Mintz, *Gouverneur Morris and the American Revolution* (Norman: University of Oklahoma Press, 1970), p. 185.

7. Ibid.

8. Farrand, p. 511.

9. Gaillard Hunt and James Brown Scott, eds., *The Debates in the Federal Convention of 1787 Which Framed the Constitution of the United States of America* (New York: Oxford University Press, 1920), pp. 202–203.

Chapter 7. Free or Slave, President or King?

1. Gaillard Hunt and James Brown Scott, eds., *The Debates in the Federal Convention of 1787 Which Framed the Constitution of the United States of America* (New York: Oxford University Press, 1920), p. 360.

2. Ibid.

3. Ibid.

4. Max Farrand, ed., *The Records of the Federal Convention of 1787, four volumes* (New Haven, Conn.: Yale University Press, 1937), vol. 2, p. 53.

5. Ibid., p. 33.

6. Ibid., p. 293.

Chapter 8. We the People

1. Max Farrand, ed., *The Records of the Federal Convention of 1787, four volumes* (New Haven, Conn.: Yale University Press, 1937), vol. 2, p. 547.

2. Ibid., p. 565.

3. Ibid., p. 590.

4. George Billias, *Elbridge Gerry: Founding Father and Republican Statesman* (New York: McGraw-Hill, 1976), pp. 199–200.

Chapter 9. American Abroad

1. Max M. Mintz, *Gouverneur Morris and the American Revolution* (Norman: University of Oklahoma Press, 1970), p. 205.

2. Jared Sparks, ed., *The Life of Gouverneur Morris, with Selections from His Correspondence and Miscellaneous Papers* (Boston: Gray & Brown, 1832), vol. 1, p. 311.

3. Ibid., p. 319.

4. Mintz, pp. 210–211.

5. Ibid., pp. 214–215.

6. Sparks, pp. 369–371.

7. Vincent Cronin, *Louis and Antoinette* (New York: William Morrow and Co., 1975), p. 373.

8. Sparks, pp. 369–371.

9. Mintz, p. 226.

Chapter 10. Last Years

1. U.S. Congress, *Biographical Directory of the American Congress, 1774–1961* (Washington, D.C.: U.S. Government Printing Office, 1961), pp. 1359–1360.

2. Max M. Mintz, *Gouverneur Morris and the American Revolution* (Norman: University of Oklahoma Press, 1970), pp. 232–233.

3. Thomas Fleming, *Duel: Alexander Hamilton, Aaron Burr and the Future of America* (New York: Basic Books, 1999), p. 333.

4. Mintz, p. 234.

5. Harold C. Syrett, ed., *The Papers of Alexander Hamilton* (New York: Columbia University Press, 1979), vol. 26, pp. 325–328.

6. Eleanor Young, *Forgotten Patriot, Robert Morris* (New York: Macmillan, 1950), p. 258.

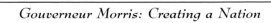

7. Alan Pell Crawford, *Unwise Passions: A True Story of a Remarkable Woman and the First Great Scandal of Eighteenth-Century America* (New York: Simon & Schuster, 2000), pp. 196–198.

8. Mintz, p. 235.

9. Crawford, p. 221.

10. *Papers of Gouverneur Morris*, Library of Congress, microfilm.

11. Theodore Roosevelt, *Gouverneur Morris* (Boston: Houghton Mifflin and Company, 1888), pp. 363–364.

Glossary

alliance—An agreement signed by two countries for the benefit of both parties.

amendment—An alteration proposed or enacted by parliamentary or constitutional procedure.

aristocrat—A member of the upper class, or nobility.

charter—A written grant of rights made by a government or ruler to an individual.

checks and balances—A system set up by the Constitution in which the executive, legislative, and judicial branches of government have the power to check each other to maintain a balance of power.

commerce—The buying or selling of goods.

compromise—A settlement in which each side gives up some of its demands.

democracy—A type of government in which the people ideally have a high degree of control over political leaders.

diplomatic—To be tactful and skillful in dealing with people.

federal—Relating to a central government.

legislator—A lawmaker.

monarchy—A government by a single person, such as a king.

negotiate—To arrange or bring about something through discussion.

orator—A public speaker.

radical—Extreme.

ratify—To approve formally.

republic—A type of government in which voters elect representatives to make the laws for the country.

shilling—A coin used in colonial America.

sovereign—One who exercises supreme authority.

tribune—An official in ancient Rome elected to protect the rights of the lower class.

unanimous—Showing total agreement.

Further Reading

Books

Adams, William Howard. *Gouverneur Morris: An Independent Life*. New Haven, Conn.: Yale University Press, 2003.

Collier, Christopher, and James Lincoln Collier. *Creating the Constitution: 1787*. Tarrytown, N.Y.: Marshall Cavendish Corporation, 1999.

King, David C. *Saratoga*. Brookfield, Conn.: Twenty-First Century Books, Inc., 1998.

Leebrick, Kristal. *The Constitution*. Mankato, Minn.: Capstone Press, Inc., 2002.

Moehn, Heather. *The U.S. Constitution: A Primary Source Investigation into the Fundamental Law of the United States*. New York: The Rosen Publishing Group, Inc., 2003.

Stein, R. Conrad. *Valley Forge*. Danbury, Conn.: Scholastic Library Publishing, 1999.

Internet Addresses

About, Inc. "Revolutionary War." *American History*. © 2002. <http://americanhistory.about.com/cs/revolutionarywar/>.

Colonial Hall. "Gouverneur Morris 1752–1816." *A Look at America's Founders*. November 28, 2002. <http://www.colonialhall.com/morrisg/morrisg.asp>.

The Library of Congress. "Jump Back in Time: Revolutionary Period (1764–1789)." *America's Story from America's Library*. n.d. <http://www.americaslibrary.gov/cgi-bin/page.cgi/jb/revolut>.

Places to Visit

Fraunces Tavern Museum
54 Pearl Street
New York, New York 10004
(212) 425-1776
<http://www.frauncestavernmuseum.org>

Independence National Historical Park
313 Walnut Street
Philadelphia, PA 19106
(215) 597-8974 visitor center

Senate House Museum
312 Fair Street
Kingston, New York 12401-3836
(845) 338-2786

Valley Forge National Historical Park
600 West Germantown Pike
Plymouth Meeting, PA 19462
1-888-VISIT-VF
<http://valleyforge.org/vfhome.asp>

Index